OLD TESTAMENT · OLD TESTAMENT · OLD TESTAMENT · OLD TESTAMENT · OLD TESTAMENT ·

THE GREAT BIBLE DISCOVERY

BEGINNINGS

The Bible is a best-seller. It is also one of the master-works of world literature - so important that universities today teach 'non-religious' Bible courses to help students who choose to study Western literature.

The Bible possesses an amazing power to fascinate young and old alike.

One reason for this universal appeal is that it deals with basic human longings, emotions, relationships. 'All the world is here.' Another reason is that so much of the Bible consists of stories. They are full of meaning but easy to remember.

Here are those stories, presented simply and with a minimum of explanation. We have left the text to speak for itself. Gifted artists use the action-strip technique to bring the Bible's deep message to readers of all ages. Their drawings are based on information from archaeological discoveries covering fifteen centuries.

An ancient book - presented for the people of the second millennium. A religious book - presented free from the interpretation of any particular church. A universal book - presented in a form that all may enjoy.

OM publishing
CARLISLE, UK

1

BEGINNINGS · BEGINNINGS · BEGINNINGS · BEGINNINGS · BEGIN

BEGINNINGS

Every family, tribe and nation has its own stories about 'where we came from'. The human family has its own immense questions: how did the world begin? why is it the way it is? who invented farming - shepherding? why do people speak so many different languages? The people of the ancient world - Egyptians, Assyrians, Babylonians - had their own answers. The Book of Genesis contains the stories God gave to the Hebrews in order to answer their questions.

In these stories we see a God who is wise, powerful and loving. Out of chaos he creates order. He calls into existence the immense variety of stars, plants, animals. He invents marriage. The creatures he forms 'in his image' are themselves capable of wonderful achievements. They cultivate the soil, breed animals, build cities. But there is in them an evil impulse which is hostile to God's goodness and leads them to oppress and exploit one another.

Genesis sees God's justice in judgements such as the Flood and the destruction of Sodom. It sees his love in the way he creates all things, in his saving Noah and his family and later choosing Abraham.

The God of the Bible is infinite in power and wisdom. Yet he is also personal. He speaks with men and women. One biblical writer refers to Abraham as 'God's friend'. Genesis begins the story of how God worked to achieve friendship with human beings whose attitude to him is often one of fear and resentment.

Abraham is one of the most important people in the history of salvation. His story tells how God made a new beginning after humankind was devastated by the Flood and divided at Babel. He spoke to Abraham and Abraham responded in faith. Nobody knows just how. Ur was an important and prosperous city but for some reason Abraham decided to leave it. Genesis 12:1 simply - and mysteriously - says that God told him to. The story on pages 27-30 does not appear in the Bible. Perhaps Abraham did reach his great decision in this way. Or perhaps not.

The Hebrew tribes were descended from Abraham, the entire Old Testament history and religion goes back to him. His trust in God remains a pattern of what faith should be.

GENESIS 1-18

First published as *Découvrir la Bible* 1983

First edition © Librairie Larousse 1983
English translation © Daan Retief Publishers 1990
24-volume series adaptation by Mike Jacklin © Knowledge Unlimited 1994
This edition © OM Publishing 1995

01 00 99 98 97 96 95   7 6 5 4 3 2 1

OM Publishing is an imprint of Send the Light Ltd.,
P.O. Box 300, Carlisle, Cumbria CA3 0QS, U.K.

All rights reserved.
No part of this publication may be reproduced, stored in a retrieval system, or transmitted, in any form or by any means, electronic, mechanical, photocopying, recording or otherwise, without the prior permission of the publishers.

Series editor: D. Roy Briggs
English translation: Bethan Uden
Introductions: Peter Cousins

British Library Cataloguing in Publication Data
A catalogue record for this book is available from the British Library
ISBN 1-85078-205-9

Printed in Singapore by Tien Wah Press (Pte) Ltd.

THE CREATION

SOMEWHERE IN THE GREAT CITY OF BABYLON A JEWISH FAMILY GETS READY TO CELEBRATE THE SABBATH.

"FATHER, THEY SAY THAT THE SABBATH **CELEBRATES THE CREATION**... CAN YOU EXPLAIN THAT TO US?"

"OH YES! TELL US AGAIN HOW GOD MADE EVERYTHING."

"LISTEN CAREFULLY. IN THE BEGINNING GOD MADE HEAVEN AND EARTH. THE EARTH WAS NOTHING BUT "TOHU-BOHU": DESERT, CHAOS..."

AND THE SPIRIT OF GOD HOVERED OVER THE SURFACE OF THE WATERS.

THE FESTIVAL OF THE SABBATH BEGINS AT SUNSET. MOTHER BRINGS THE LIGHT.

GOD SAID, **'LET THERE BE LIGHT'** ... AND THE LIGHT APPEARED.

GOD SAW THAT THE LIGHT WAS GOOD, AND HE SEPARATED THE LIGHT FROM THE DARKNESS. HE NAMED THE LIGHT **'DAY'** AND THE DARKNESS **'NIGHT'**.

THERE WAS EVENING AND THEN MORNING; **THAT WAS THE FIRST DAY.**

GOD SAID, 'LET THERE BE A SPACE IN BETWEEN THE WATERS.' AND HE SEPARATED THE WATERS UNDER IT FROM THE WATERS ABOVE IT. GOD NAMED THE SPACE **'SKY'**.

GOD COMMANDED, 'LET THE WATERS BELOW COME TOGETHER IN ONE PLACE AND LET LAND APPEAR!' HE NAMED THE LAND **'EARTH'** AND THE WATERS GATHERED TOGETHER HE NAMED **'SEA'**.

GOD SAW THAT IT WAS GOOD.

GOD SAID, 'LET THE EARTH PRODUCE PLANTS BEARING GRAIN AND TREES BEARING FRUIT, EACH ACCORDING TO ITS OWN KIND.'

GOD SAW THAT IT WAS GOOD.

SECOND DAY

THIRD DAY

God said, 'Let lights appear in the sky to separate day and night.' And it was done. **God saw that it was good.**

FOURTH DAY

God said, 'Let the waters be filled with many kinds of living beings. Let the air be filled with birds.' **God saw that it was good.**

Then, my children, God commanded the fish to reproduce and fill the seas and the birds to increase in number on the land.

FIFTH DAY

God said, 'Let the earth produce living beings according to their different kinds.' And it was done. **God saw that it was good.**

God said, 'Now let us make human beings — in our image.' He created them in his image, male and female.

SIXTH DAY
GOD SAID TO THEM, 'HAVE MANY CHILDREN AND FILL THE EARTH. YOU ARE IN CHARGE OF IT. RULE OVER ALL THE ANIMALS.'
AND GOD BLESSED THE SEVENTH DAY AND SET IT APART BECAUSE BY THAT DAY HE HAD COMPLETED HIS CREATION AND STOPPED WORKING.
THAT IS WHY WE CELEBRATE THE SABBATH. IT HAS BEEN GIVEN TO US AS AN INHERITANCE, SO THAT WE CAN SHARE THE JOY OF CREATION.
BUT, FATHER, MANY OTHER THINGS ARE TOLD ABOUT THE CREATION...
SURE!
LISTEN TO WHAT MY GRANDFATHER SHLOMO TOLD ME WHEN WE WERE IN OUR OWN LAND. I CAN STILL HEAR HIM SPEAKING!

WHEN THE LORD MADE EARTH AND HEAVEN, THERE WERE STILL NO TREES OR PLANTS ON THE EARTH. GOD HAD NOT YET MADE RAIN.
THEN WATER GUSHED OUT OF THE SOIL, AND GOD TOOK SOME CLAY AND MADE A MAN FROM IT; HE BREATHED LIFE-GIVING BREATH INTO HIS NOSTRILS.
AND THE MAN BEGAN TO LIVE.
THEN THE LORD GOD PLANTED A GARDEN IN EDEN, AND PUT THE MAN THERE TO CULTIVATE IT AND LOOK AFTER IT.
THE LORD GOD SAID TO THE MAN, 'YOU MAY EAT THE FRUIT OF ALL THE TREES EXCEPT OF THE TREE WHICH GIVES KNOWLEDGE OF GOOD AND EVIL!
IF YOU EAT THAT FRUIT, YOU WILL DIE.'

YOU KNOW WHAT HAPPENED NEXT, HOW THE MAN DISOBEYED GOD...
THAT DOES NOT MATTER, SHLOMO! TELL US AGAIN!
GOOD... BUT THIS TIME YOU'RE GOING TO HELP ME. JOEL, YOU'LL BE ADAM. ESTHER, YOU'LL BE THE WOMAN.
AND YES, SHLOMO, YOU PLAY THE PART OF THE LORD GOD.
IT'S NOT GOOD FOR MAN TO LIVE ALONE! I'LL FIND HIM A HELPER.
HERE ARE THE ANIMALS I'VE MADE. YOU MUST GIVE THEM NAMES BECAUSE THEY'RE YOURS.
PORCUPINE! OWL! DRAGONFLY!
I'M NOT ALONE ANY MORE, BUT THERE'S NO ONE LIKE ME.

LEAVE IT TO ME!
I TAKE ONE OF HIS RIBS AND...
LOOK!
AT LAST, HERE'S ONE OF MY OWN KIND, BONE FROM MY BONE, AND FLESH FROM MY FLESH.
WE BELONG TO EACH OTHER, AND EVERYTHING'S OURS!
'EVERYTHING EXCEPT THE FORBIDDEN TREE!' SAID THE SNAKE, THE MOST CUNNING OF ALL THE ANIMALS.
YES, IT BRINGS DEATH!

NOW THEN, IF YOU EAT IT, YOU'LL BE LIKE THE GODS, KNOWING WHAT'S GOOD AND WHAT'S BAD.
HERE – YOU HAVE SOME TOO!
THEY BOTH ATE IT. THEN, AT DUSK...
ADAM! ADAM!
WHEN I HEARD YOUR VOICE, I WAS FRIGHTENED AND I HID MYSELF.
FRIGHTENED OF ME? HAVE YOU EATEN THE FRUIT OF THE FORBIDDEN TREE?
IT WAS THE WOMAN YOU GAVE TO ME WHO...
THE SNAKE TRICKED ME...
SNAKE, YOU ARE CURSED! YOU'LL EAT DUST ALL YOUR LIFE. THE WOMAN'S CHILDREN WILL CRUSH YOUR HEAD AND YOU WILL BITE THEIR HEEL.

LOOK AT ADAM AND EVE... CHASED OUT OF THE GARDEN. LET'S GO BACK TO THE CAMP.
SINCE THAT DAY **IT'S BEEN A STRUGGLE FOR MEN AND WOMEN TO SURVIVE,** RIGHT UP UNTIL THEY DIE.
BUT, SHLOMO, **EVERYTHING COULD HAVE ENDED THERE!**
YES, BUT GOD GAVE HUMAN BEINGS A CHANCE. HE LET THEM HAVE DESCENDANTS. **I'LL TELL YOU THE WHOLE STORY.**
ADAM AND EVE HAD TWO SONS. **CAIN**, THE ELDEST, WAS A FARMER...

ABEL, THE SECOND, WAS A SHEPHERD.
LORD, YOU HAVE SO MANY THINGS. HOW WISELY YOU MADE THEM ALL. THE EARTH IS FILLED WITH YOUR CREATURES. Psalm 104
ONE DAY, CAIN BROUGHT AN OFFERING
TO GOD...
AND ABEL DID THE SAME.
ALL-POWERFUL GOD, GIVE ME A GOOD HARVEST...
MY GOD, I WANT TO THANK YOU... ACCEPT THE FIRST-BORN OF MY FLOCK...
HAIL! THAT'S GOD'S ANSWER! MY HARVEST'S LOST!
THE LORD GIVES LIFE. HOW WONDERFUL!

I'M SO SORRY. YOUR HARVEST WAS LOOKING GOOD.
YOU'RE GOING TO PAY ME FOR IT!
THIS TIME GOD DIDN'T PROTECT YOU!
THE LORD HAD ONLY TO ACCEPT MY OFFERING. AFTER ALL, IT'S HIS FAULT THAT I KILLED ABEL!
OLD SHLOMO WENT ON WITH HIS STORY...
THE LORD SAID TO CAIN, 'WHERE'S YOUR BROTHER ABEL?'

"I DON'T KNOW! AM I SUPPOSED TO TAKE CARE OF MY BROTHER?"

"WHAT HAVE YOU DONE? YOUR BROTHER'S BLOOD IS CRYING OUT TO ME."

THEY HUNG ON SHLOMO'S EVERY WORD...

"NOW YOU'RE CURSED. WHEN YOU CULTIVATE THE SOIL, IT WON'T GIVE ITS RICHES TO YOU. YOU'LL BE A HOMELESS WANDERER ON THE EARTH."

"BUT THAT'S IMPOSSIBLE! YOU CHASE ME OUT OF THIS LAND, **AND I CAN'T HIDE AWAY FROM YOU!**"

"I'LL BE A HOMELESS WANDERER ON THE EARTH, AND THE FIRST PERSON I MEET WILL KILL ME."

THEN THE LORD PROMISED TO PROTECT CAIN FROM HIS ENEMIES.

WHERE COULD I GO TO ESCAPE FROM YOU? WHERE COULD I GET AWAY FROM YOUR PRESENCE?

psalm 139

CAIN HAD A SON, **ENOCH**. HE BUILT HIM A TOWN.

THERE'S YOUR KINGDOM... AND THAT'S ONLY THE BEGINNING.

ONE OF ENOCH'S DESCENDANTS WAS NAMED **LAMECH**...

AND I SAY, WHILE THERE IS LIFE, THERE MUST BE PLEASURE.

LAMECH HAD THREE SONS. HE TAUGHT THE FIRST, JABAL, ABOUT **GAIN AND PROFIT**.

TO FATTEN A HERD YOU MUST KNOW HOW TO CHANGE THEIR PASTURE.

HE TAUGHT JUBAL, THE SECOND, **MUSIC**.

JUBAL, YOU SING LIKE A GOD!

AGAIN...! EVERYTHING YOU SING IS SO LOVELY.

HE TAUGHT THE THIRD, TUBAL-CAIN, TO MAKE **WEAPONS**.

EVE HAD ANOTHER SON, WHOM SHE CALLED SETH. HE TOOK ABEL'S PLACE IN HER HEART.

"EVERYTHING COMES FROM GOD. EVERYTHING IS WONDERFUL."

FROM THERE IT WAS ONLY A STEP TO WORSHIPPING THE CREATURES GOD HAD MADE...

... SOMETHING SETH'S DESCENDANTS DID...

"O SUN, KING OF HEAVEN, BE BLESSED! YOU SHED YOUR LIGHT ON US AGAIN THIS MORNING."

NOAH

METHUSELAH

ENOCH

BUT AMONG HIS DESCENDANTS ENOCH, METHUSELAH AND NOAH WENT ON WORSHIPPING GOD THE CREATOR OF ALL THINGS

THE LORD SAW HOW WICKED PEOPLE HAD BECOME.

SHLOMO WAS GOING TO MAKE THAT PLAIN IN HIS STORY.

THE LORD WAS SORRY HE HAD MADE HUMAN BEINGS. THEY MADE HIM VERY SAD.

HE SAID, 'I'LL WIPE OUT THESE PEOPLE FROM THE FACE OF THE EARTH, AND WITH THEM THE ANIMALS, THE REPTILES AND THE BIRDS OF THE SKY, BECAUSE I'M SORRY THAT I MADE THEM.'

BUT ONE MAN PLEASED HIM: **NOAH**.

THE LORD SAID TO NOAH, 'THEY'VE FILLED THE WORLD WITH VIOLENCE. I'M GOING TO DESTROY THEM!

'... NOAH, MAKE AN **ARK** OF CYPRUS WOOD, AND TAKE WITH YOU A PAIR OF EVERY LIVING THING...'

'FOR MY PART, I'M GOING TO MAKE A FLOOD OF WATER FALL ON THE EARTH, AND EVERY LIVING THING THAT BREATHES WILL DISAPPEAR!'

NOAH SET TO WORK WITH HIS THREE SONS, SHEM, HAM AND JAPHETH. **HE DID EVERYTHING THAT GOD HAD ASKED OF HIM.**

... THERE! ... NOW IT ONLY NEEDS TO BE FILLED.

THEN NOAH ENTERED THE ARK WITH HIS WIFE, HIS SONS AND THEIR WIVES, AND A PAIR OF EACH ANIMAL ON EARTH.

HERE IT COMES! SPRINGS ARE GUSHING FROM A GREAT ABYSS...
ONLY NOAH KNEW WHAT WAS GOING TO HAPPEN.
... AND THE FLOODGATES OF THE SKY ARE OPEN.
AT LAST, A LITTLE RAIN ON MY FIELD! AFTER MY LONG WAIT!
... BUT THEY MOCKED NOAH...
LET US GO OUT FOR A LITTLE FRESH AIR...
THE WATER ROSE, AND THE ARK BEGAN TO FLOAT.

THE FLOOD LASTED FORTY DAYS AND FORTY NIGHTS.
WATER COVERED THE EARTH FOR 150 DAYS, THEN, LITTLE BY LITTLE, IT SUBSIDED.
NOAH, WE'RE ALL GOING TO DIE!
NO, WIFE! IT'S THE OTHERS WHO ARE DYING RIGHT NOW.
FLY AWAY! GO AND LAND ON DRY GROUND...
SOON WE SHALL BE ABLE TO LEAVE THE ARK...
BUT THE DOVE DID NOT FIND A PLACE TO LAND, AND CAME BACK TO THE ARK. SEVEN DAYS LATER NOAH SENT HER OUT AGAIN, AND THIS TIME SHE CAME BACK WITH AN OLIVE BRANCH.

LISTEN CAREFULLY TO WHAT THE LORD SAID NEXT: 'SEED TIME AND HARVEST, COLD AND HEAT, SUMMER AND WINTER, DAY AND NIGHT WILL NEVER COME TO AN END.'
NO MORE FLOODS. THIS IS THE SIGN...
... OF MY COVENANT
LET MY OFFERING PLEASE YOU, LORD.
AS SOON AS HE LEFT THE ARK WITH HIS FAMILY, NOAH OFFERED A SACRIFICE...
I AM MAKING WITH YOU AND WITH EVERYTHING THAT LIVES. PEOPLE, THE WHOLE EARTH...
JAPHETH
HAM
SHEM
FROM SHEM, HAM AND JAPHETH, THE SONS OF NOAH, COME ALL THE PEOPLES OF THE EARTH.

AT THAT TIME EVERYBODY SPOKE THE SAME LANGUAGE. THEY SETTLED ON A PLAIN TO THE EAST.
THEN THEY HAD AN IDEA...
LET'S GET TOGETHER. WE'LL BE STRONGER TO COPE WITH NATURAL DISASTERS.
AND THE GODS WON'T BE ABLE TO DO ANYTHING AGAINST US.
IT WILL BE GOOD TO LIVE TOGETHER!
LET'S BUILD A CITY. LET'S BUILD A TOWER WITH ITS TOP TOUCHING THE SKY.
AND WE'LL BE A FORCE TO BE RECKONED WITH!
THEN THE LORD CAME DOWN TO SEE WHAT THE PEOPLE WERE BUILDING...

...AND HE DECIDED TO PUT AN END TO THEIR PLAN.
BUT WHY, SHLOMO?
BECAUSE ONCE AGAIN HUMAN BEINGS WERE RELYING ON THEIR OWN STRENGTH.
THAT CITY WAS BUILT ONLY ON SELFISHNESS AND THE LUST FOR AUTHORITY AND POWER.
THE LORD JUMBLED UP THEIR LANGUAGE...
TOGETHER WE ARE MASTERS OF THE UNIVERSE!
...AND SCATTERED THEM THROUGHOUT THE EARTH.
ALONE...
ALONE...
ALONE...

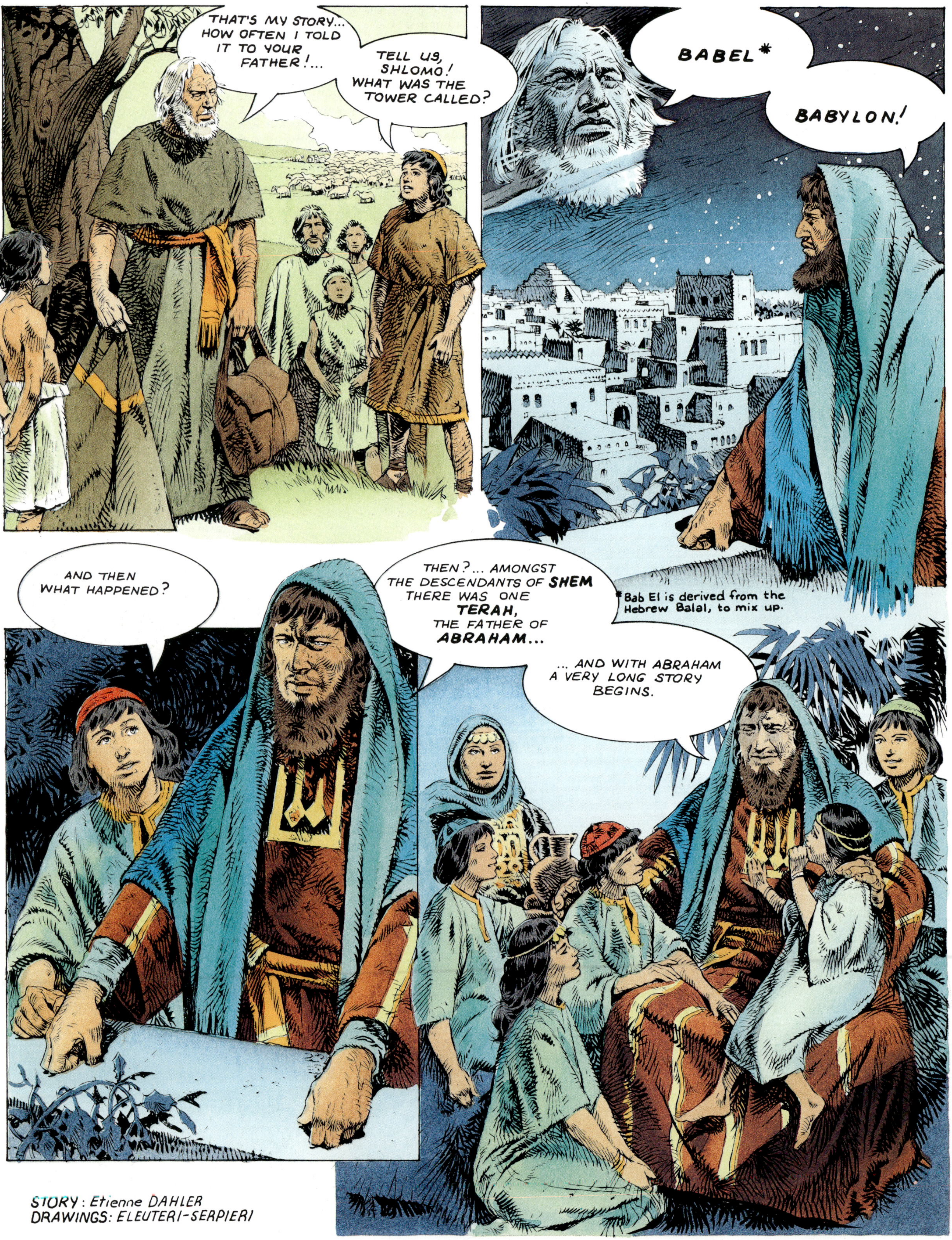

STORY: Etienne DAHLER
DRAWINGS: ELEUTERI-SERPIERI

ABRAHAM

ONE DAY, A LONG TIME AGO—SOME 3500 YEARS AGO...

...TWO TRAVELLERS WENT ON FOOT TO THE LAND OF THE EUPHRATES, TOWARDS THE GREAT CITY OF **UR**...

STORY: Etienne DAHLER
DRAWINGS: Victor de la FUENTE

LET'S GO AND GREET TERAH!

MAY THE GODS PROTECT YOU!

MAY SIN* GO WITH YOU!

*The moon-god.

WE HAVE COME FOR THE FESTIVALS.
THEY BEGIN TONIGHT.
WILL WE SEE YOUR SONS ABRAM AND NAHOR THERE?
NAHOR, FOR SURE... ABRAM, I DON'T KNOW. JUST RECENTLY HE'S BEEN THINKING TOO MUCH...
THAT EVENING...
SIN! PROTECT US!
ENLIL! HEAL MY CHILD!
ISHTAR! LET THE HARVEST BE GOOD!
TO THINK THEY'RE WORSHIPPING THINGS THEY'VE MADE THEMSELVES!

THE PLANETS, THE STARS, THE VAST SKY...
...THE EARTH AND EVERYTHING IN IT... THEIR GODS MEAN NOTHING!
SARAI, I'M CONVINCED... THERE'S AN ALMIGHTY GOD WHO RULES OVER EVERYTHING...
HE'S NOT THE MOON, NOR THE SUN ... HE'S MUCH HIGHER...
BUT WHAT'S HIS NAME?
I DON'T KNOW IT YET... BUT I'M SURE OF ONE THING...
OH! IF ONLY THOSE AROUND US KNEW HIM!

NOT IN BIBLE

Panel 1: "LOOK HERE, THIS IS WHAT I BELIEVE... YOU MUST DO WHAT SEEMS BEST TO YOU."

Panel 2: "WHAT YOU SAY ECHOES IN MY HEART..." / "I HAVE BEEN EXPECTING THIS FOR A LONG TIME!"

Panel 3: A FEW DAYS LATER... "NOW WE MUST PRAY TO ALMIGHTY GOD..."

Panel 4: "HE'LL ANSWER— SOONER OR LATER..."

Panel 5: SOON AFTERWARDS IN TERAH'S SHOP... "STOP!" / "THIS JOKE'S LASTED LONG ENOUGH!" / "YOUR GODS ARE WORTHLESS!" / "YOU'VE GONE MAD!"

ABRAM, MY SON, AFTER YOUR OUTBURST, THE KING SENT FOR ME...
... HE'D LIKE TO FORGET WHAT HAPPENED, BUT...
... WE HAVE 2 DAYS TO LEAVE THE CITY.
FORGIVE ME, FATHER.
SARAI, WE'VE GOT TO LEAVE UR...
THE CARAVAN TOOK THE ROAD TO THE NORTH WEST.
ABRAM, TAKE THE LEAD! LOT, MY NEPHEW, BRING UP THE REAR!

NOT IN BIBLE

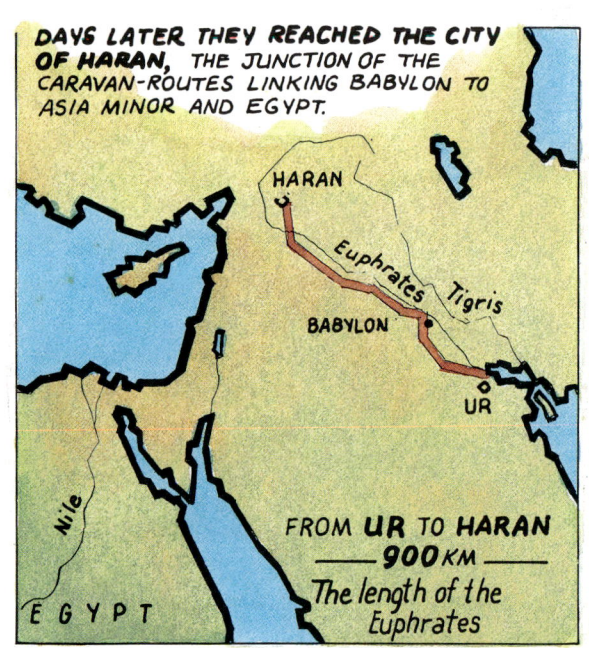

DAYS LATER THEY REACHED THE CITY OF HARAN, THE JUNCTION OF THE CARAVAN-ROUTES LINKING BABYLON TO ASIA MINOR AND EGYPT. FROM UR TO HARAN — 900 KM — The length of the Euphrates	"THIS PLACE IS MADE FOR TRADE... LET'S STAY HERE!" "YES, TERAH... WE NEEDN'T GO ANY FURTHER."

IN THE CAMP...

"YESTERDAY EVENING THERE WERE 300 OF US, AND ABRAM'S WORD WAS STRONGER THAN EVER."

"I'VE THE FEELING THAT SOMETHING IMPORTANT'S ABOUT TO HAPPEN."

לֶךְ־לְךָ מֵאַרְצְךָ וּמִמּוֹלַדְתְּךָ וּמִבֵּית אָבִיךָ אֶל־הָאָרֶץ אֲשֶׁר אַרְאֶךָּ *

*LEAVE YOUR COUNTRY, YOUR FAMILY AND YOUR FATHER'S HOUSE, AND GO TO THE LAND I WILL SHOW YOU.

ABRAM LEFT, AS GOD HAD COMMANDED HIM.

WE'VE ARRIVED! HOW WONDERFUL!
BUT... OTHER PEOPLE LIVE HERE!
LOT, LET'S GO ON EXPLORING THIS LAND.
IN THE JORDAN VALLEY...
IT SEEMS THERE'S NO SPACE FOR US!
ALL THE GOOD LAND'S ALREADY BEEN TAKEN!
LORD, I DON'T UNDERSTAND ANY MORE.
לְזַרְעֲךָ אֶתֵּן אֶת־הָאָרֶץ הַזֹּאת*
* I WILL GIVE THIS LAND TO YOUR DESCENDANTS.

GUARD, LET ME ALSO PUT UP AN ALTAR TO MY GOD.
AT SHECHEM, HOLY PLACE OF THE CANAANITES...
MAY THIS PLACE REMIND US OF YOUR PROMISE.
THEN THE CARAVAN CONTINUED SOUTHWARDS TOWARDS THE DESERT...
DEATH WAITS FOR US HERE!
ONLY ONE CHOICE: EGYPT. FAMINE NEVER REACHES THE NILE.
WE'RE NEAR EGYPT... YOU'RE BEAUTIFUL, SARAI, AND THE EGYPTIANS WILL NOTICE YOU... TELL THEM YOU'RE MY SISTER, THEN THEY'LL LET ME LIVE.
THIS IS THE PRICE OF KEEPING GOD'S PROMISE SAFE.

WE'VE COME FROM CANAAN WHERE THERE IS A BAD FAMINE...
AND YOU THINK EGYPT WILL FEED ALL THESE PEOPLE!
ABOUT TURN! BACK WHERE YOU CAME FROM!
WAIT A MINUTE!
CHIEF, THERE'S A CARAVAN ASKING FOR HELP... WITH SUCH A BEAUTIFUL WOMAN...
WELL, NOW! LET'S GO AND SEE...
YOU'VE A VERY BEAUTIFUL WIFE!
YOU'RE MISTAKEN, SIR. SARAI IS MY SISTER.
GOOD! GO AHEAD!

MASTER, SOME EGYPTIAN SOLDIERS HAVE COME WITH PRESENTS! CAMELS... SHEEP... DONKEYS...

THEY'RE ORDERED TO TAKE SARAI TO THE PHARAOH'S PALACE...

THIS WAS WHAT I FEARED, SARAI...

NEVER FEAR. I'LL SAY NOTHING.

IF THIS BEAUTY'S ALL THAT YOU SAY SHE IS, I'LL MAKE HER MY WIFE TONIGHT.

A FEW HOURS LATER...

THE PHARAOH MUST BE WARNED IMMEDIATELY...

TOO LATE!

35

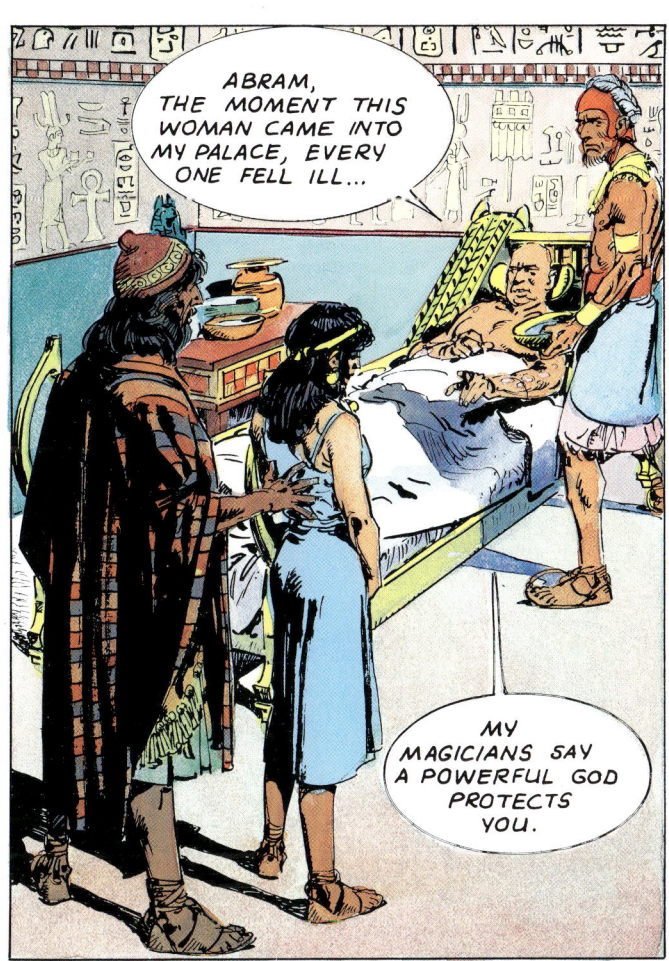

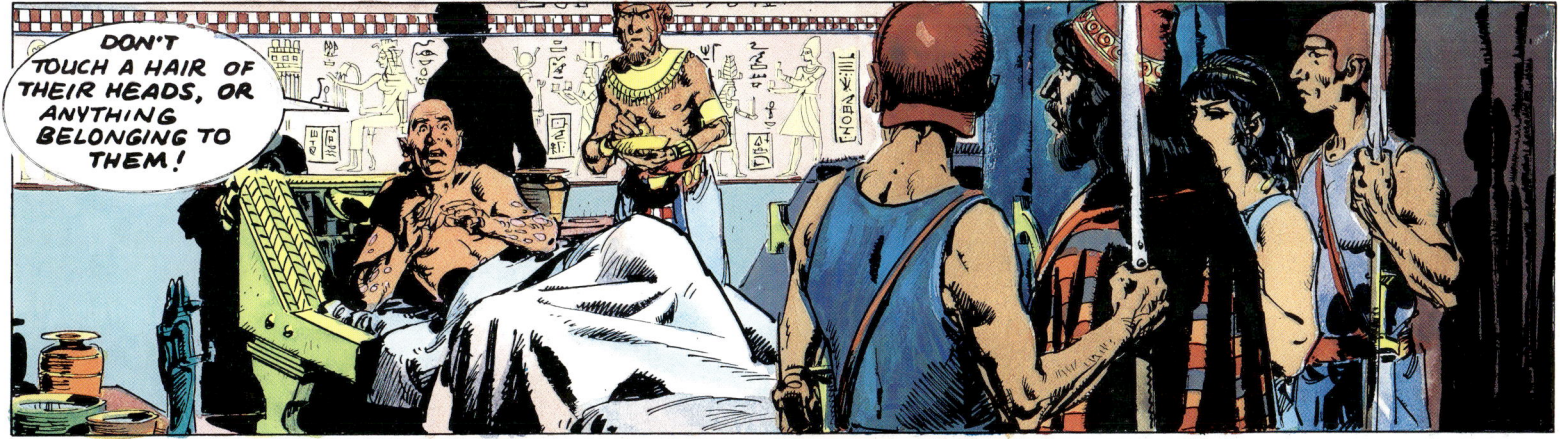

FROM EGYPT, ABRAM RETRACED HIS STEPS ACROSS THE NEGEB DESERT. BUT LOT'S SHEPHERDS...
THE ANIMALS DON'T HAVE ENOUGH TO EAT!
SOON WE'LL HAVE NO MORE MILK...
ABRAM'S FLOCKS ARE TOO BIG!
LET'S MUZZLE THE ANIMALS EVERY OTHER DAY, SO THEY DON'T DIE.
I, LOT, AM THE SOLE HEIR OF ABRAM! IT'S MY INHERITANCE HE IS SPOILING...
YES, OUT OF JEALOUSY BECAUSE HE DOES NOT HAVE A CHILD!
ALL THE LAND YOU SEE I WILL GIVE TO YOU AND YOUR DESCENDANTS FOREVER.
THIS PROMISE WAS MADE TO ABRAM...

37

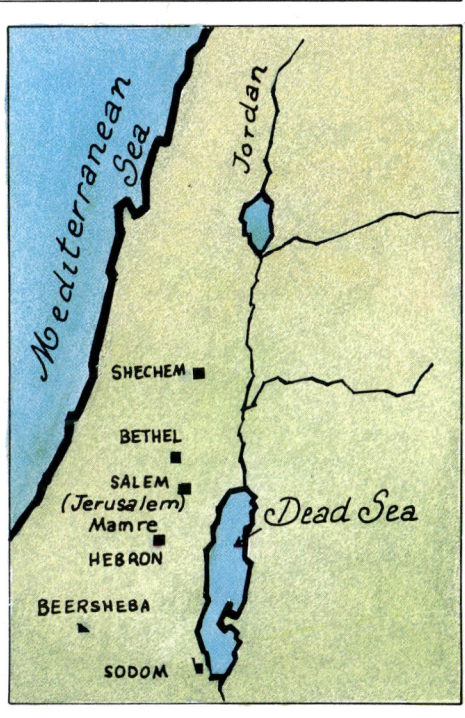

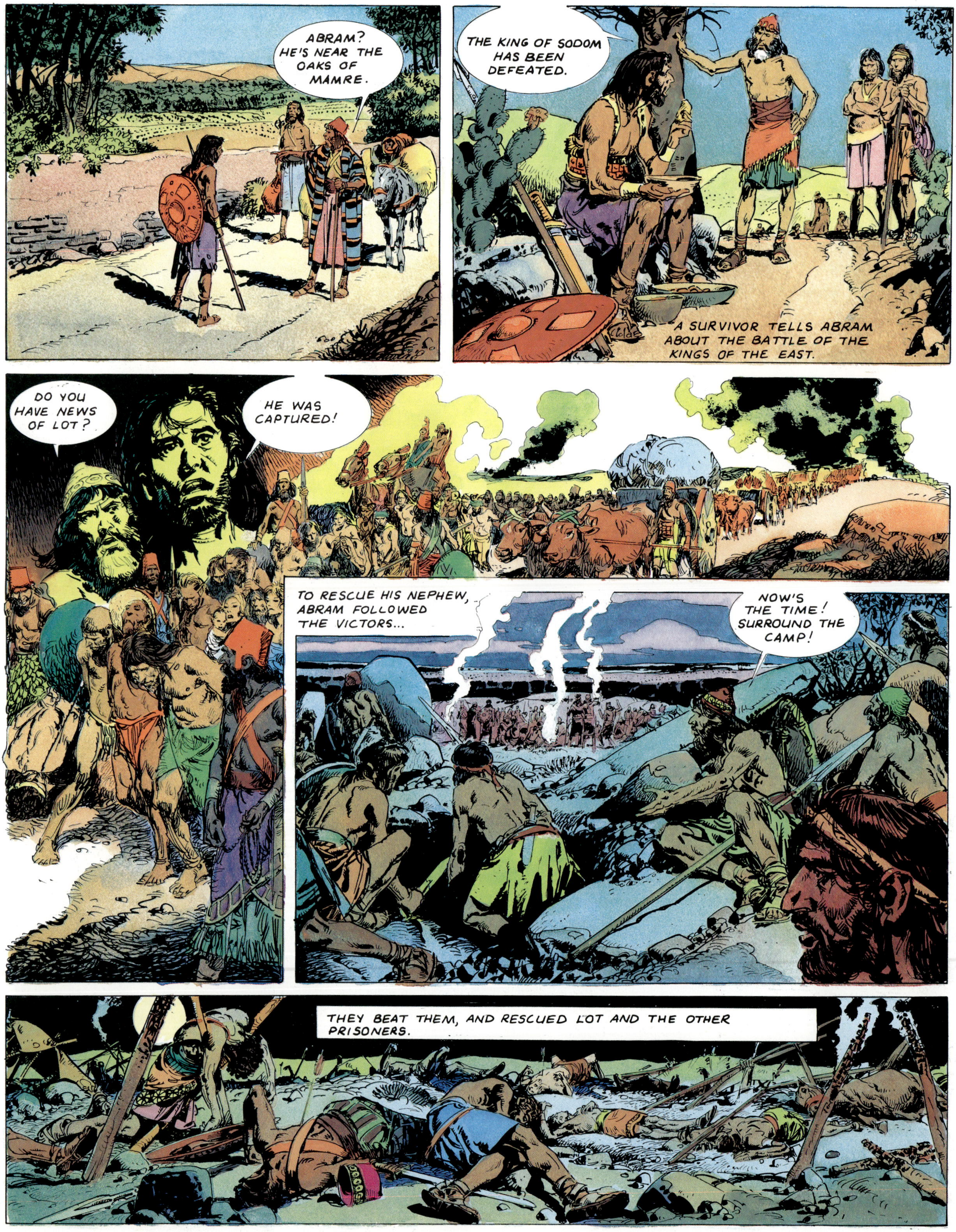
ABRAM? HE'S NEAR THE OAKS OF MAMRE.
THE KING OF SODOM HAS BEEN DEFEATED.
A SURVIVOR TELLS ABRAM ABOUT THE BATTLE OF THE KINGS OF THE EAST.
DO YOU HAVE NEWS OF LOT?
HE WAS CAPTURED!
TO RESCUE HIS NEPHEW, ABRAM FOLLOWED THE VICTORS...
NOW'S THE TIME! SURROUND THE CAMP!
THEY BEAT THEM, AND RESCUED LOT AND THE OTHER PRISONERS.

ON THE ROAD BACK, ABRAM HEADED TOWARDS SALEM, THE FUTURE JERUSALEM, WHERE MELCHIZEDEK WAS KING.

IT'S ABRAM! HE'S DEFEATED THE KINGS OF THE EAST.

LET'S GO TO MEET HIM...

MELCHIZEDEK TOOK HIM BREAD AND WINE...

YOU'RE BLESSED, ABRAM! ALMIGHTY GOD GAVE YOU VICTORY.

SOME TIME LATER ABRAM THOUGHT ABOUT THE BATTLE...
THERE WERE SURELY GOOD PEOPLE AMONGST THOSE WE KILLED. THE SURVIVORS WILL TRY TO AVENGE THEM...
DON'T BE AFRAID, ABRAM. I AM YOUR SHIELD; YOUR REWARD WILL BE GREAT.
COUNT THE STARS, IF YOU CAN... THAT WILL BE THE NUMBER OF YOUR DESCENDANTS.
ABRAM BEGGED HIS GOD TO GIVE HIM A SON.

BUT SARAI STILL HAD NO CHILDREN.
ABRAM, I WILL NEVER HAVE A CHILD.
HAGAR, MY SLAVE-GIRL, COULD GIVE YOU ONE...
YOU MUST HAVE AN HEIR!

AFTER A FEW MONTHS, HAGAR, THE EGYPTIAN, WAS PREGNANT WITH ABRAM'S CHILD.
I, THE SLAVE-GIRL, AM BLESSED BY GOD! I SHAN'T BE A SLAVE FOR MUCH LONGER!
I'LL DO NOTHING BUT CARRY ABRAM'S CHILD!
HAGAR, YOU'LL NEVER BE MORE THAN A SLAVE!
SARAI TREATED HER IN SUCH A HUMILIATING WAY THAT HAGAR RAN AWAY FROM HER...

HAGAR, WHERE ARE YOU GOING?
GO BACK TO YOUR MISTRESS AND GIVE IN TO HER.
YOU'LL HAVE A SON. YOU MUST NAME HIM ISHMAEL!
HE'LL BE AGAINST EVERY ONE. EVERY ONE WILL BE AGAINST HIM.

SO HAGAR RETURNED TO ABRAM'S CLAN. THE PROMISE CAME TRUE...

WE'LL MARK OUR BODIES TO SHOW THAT WE BELONG TO GOD.

ISHMAEL, YOU'LL BE THE FIRST TO BE CIRCUMCISED.

ISHMAEL GREW IN THE SHADOW OF HIS FATHER.

FROM NOW MY NAME WILL BE **ABRAHAM**, FOR I'LL BE THE FATHER OF A MULTITUDE.

AND SARAI WILL BE **SARAH**, THE PRINCESS, MOTHER OF KINGS.

ONE DAY AT HIGH NOON...

AM I DREAMING?

LORD! I BEG YOU, DON'T PASS BY WITHOUT STOP-PING!
REFRESH YOURSELVES...
SARAH, QUICKLY - CAKES!... I'LL CHOOSE THE TENDEREST CALF.
WHERE'S YOUR WIFE, SARAH?
IN THE TENT!
WHEN I COME BACK A YEAR FROM NOW, YOUR WIFE WILL HAVE A SON!
I'M TOO OLD! ONLY GOD CAN MAKE A PROMISE LIKE THAT.
YES, ONLY GOD!

RISING, THE THREE TRAVELLERS LOOKED TOWARDS SODOM AND GOMORRAH...

WHAT A RACKET!

THESE CITIES WERE RULED BY MONEY, PROFIT AND PLEASURE.

IF THEY BEHAVE AS PEOPLE SAY, I'LL DESTROY THEM!
LORD, WOULD YOU HAVE THE GOOD DIE WITH THE WICKED? WON'T YOU FORGIVE THEM?
THERE ARE FIVE CITIES IN THE VALLEY. IF THERE ARE 10 PEOPLE IN EACH WHO WORSHIP YOU AND BEHAVE FAIRLY?
I'LL PARDON EVERYONE BECAUSE OF THEM.
IF YOU FIND 40 SUCH PEOPLE?
I'LL DO NOTHING BECAUSE OF THOSE 40.
IF YOU FIND 30?
I'LL DO NOTHING IF I FIND 30.
AND 20?
I'LL NOT DESTROY THEM FOR THOSE 20.
10?
EVEN FOR 10, I'LL NOT DESTROY THE CITIES.